Co

by Murray Ogilvie

 Lang Syne

PUBLISHING

WRITING *to* REMEMBER

Lang**Syne**

PUBLISHING

WRITING *to* REMEMBER

79 Main Street, Newtongrange,
Midlothian EH22 4NA
Tel: 0131 344 0414
E-mail: info@lang-syne.co.uk
www.langsyneshop.co.uk

Design by Dorothy Meikle
Printed by Printwell Ltd
© Lang Syne Publishers Ltd 2023

ISBN 978-1-85217-308-1

Cochrane

SEPT NAMES:

Cochrane
Cochran
Coughran
Cocheran
Cockran
Cockrum
Cohran
Cockram
Corcoran

Cochrane

MOTTO:
Virtute Et Labore
(By valour and exertion).

CREST:
A Horse passant argent.

TERRITORY:
Renfrewshire.

Chapter one:

The origins of the clan system

by Rennie McOwan

The original Scottish clans of the Highlands and the great families of the Lowlands and Borders were gatherings of families, relatives, allies and neighbours for mutual protection against rivals or invaders.

Scotland experienced invasion from the Vikings, the Romans and English armies from the south. The Norman invasion of what is now England also had an influence on land-holding in Scotland. Some of these invaders stayed on and in time became 'Scottish'.

The word clan derives from the Gaelic language term 'clann', meaning children, and it was first used many centuries ago as communities were formed around tribal lands in glens and mountain fastnesses.

The format of clans changed over the centuries, but at its best the chief and his family held the land on behalf of all, like trustees, and the ordinary clansmen and women believed they had a blood relationship with the founder of their clan.

There were two way duties and obligations. An inadequate chief could be deposed and replaced by someone of greater ability.

Clan people had an immense pride in race. Their relationship with the chief was like adult children to a father and they had a real dignity.

The concept of clanship is very old and a more feudal notion of authority gradually crept in.

Pictland, for instance, was divided into seven principalities ruled by feudal leaders who were the strongest and most charismatic leaders of their particular groups.

By the sixth century the 'British' kingdoms of Strathclyde, Lothian and Celtic Dalriada (Argyll) had emerged and Scotland, as one nation, began to take shape in the time of King Kenneth MacAlpin.

Some chiefs claimed descent from

ancient kings which may not have been accurate in every case.

By the twelfth and thirteenth centuries the clans and families were more strongly brought under the central control of Scottish monarchs.

Lands were awarded and administered more and more under royal favour, yet the power of the area clan chiefs was still very great.

The long wars to ensure Scotland's independence against the expansionist ideas of English monarchs extended the influence of some clans and reduced the lands of others.

Those who supported Scotland's greatest king, Robert the Bruce, were awarded the territories of the families who had opposed his claim to the Scottish throne.

In the Scottish Borders country – the notorious Debatable Lands – the great families built up a ferocious reputation for providing warlike men accustomed to raiding into England and occasionally fighting one another.

Chiefs had the power to dispense justice and to confiscate lands and clan warfare produced a society where martial virtues – courage, hardiness, tenacity – were greatly admired.

Gradually the relationship between the clans and the Crown became strained as Scottish monarchs became more orientated to life in the Lowlands and, on occasion, towards England.

The Highland clans spoke a different language, Gaelic, whereas the language of Lowland Scotland and the court was Scots and in more modern times, English.

Highlanders dressed differently, had different customs, and their wild mountain land sometimes seemed almost foreign to people living in the Lowlands.

It must be emphasised that Gaelic culture was very rich and story-telling, poetry, piping, the clarsach (harp) and other music all flourished and were greatly respected.

Highland culture was different from other parts of Scotland but it was not inferior or less sophisticated.

Central Government, whether in London or Edinburgh, sometimes saw the Gaelic clans as

*"The spirit of the clan means much
to thousands of people"*

a challenge to their authority and some sent expeditions into the Highlands and west to crush the power of the Lords of the Isles.

Nevertheless, when the eighteenth century Jacobite Risings came along the cause of the Stuarts was mainly supported by Highland clans.

The word Jacobite comes from the Latin for James – Jacobus. The Jacobites wanted to restore the exiled Stuarts to the throne of Britain.

The monarchies of Scotland and England became one in 1603 when King James VI of Scotland (1st of England) gained the English throne after Queen Elizabeth died.

The Union of Parliaments of Scotland and England, the Treaty of Union, took place in 1707.

Some Highland clans, of course, and Lowland families opposed the Jacobites and supported the incoming Hanoverians.

After the Jacobite cause finally went down at Culloden in 1746 a kind of ethnic cleansing took place. The power of the chiefs was curtailed. Tartan and the pipes were banned in law.

Many emigrated, some because they

wanted to, some because they were evicted by force. In addition, many Highlanders left for the cities of the south to seek work.

Many of the clan lands became home to sheep and deer shooting estates.

But the warlike traditions of the clans and the great Lowland and Border families lived on, with their descendants fighting bravely for freedom in two world wars.

Remember the men from whence you came, says the Gaelic proverb, and to that could be added the role of many heroic women.

The spirit of the clan, of having roots, whether Highland or Lowland, means much to thousands of people.

Chapter two:

In the beginning

There are several theories surrounding the origin of the Cochrane clan. The popular belief, and one supported by many clansmen is that they began life in an area called Coueran or Coveran, which was in modern-day county of Renfrewshire, near the bustling town of Paisley. Coveran, which was a Norman name, eventually evolved into Cochrane. The very first Coveran is said to be a Norse warrior who arrived in Scotland in the ninth century with his countrymen to pillage and plunder the west coast – but decided to settle there.

Another possibility is that the name comes from the Gaelic words for "brave fellow". Legend has it that a family member who proved particularly brave and ferocious in battle was described by his commander as 'coch ran' which translates to brave fellow. Similarly coch ran could also relate to the words 'battle cry' or 'the roar of battle'.

By the thirteenth century the family, still known as Coveran, was undoubtedly one of the more prominent in the region. In 1262 Waldenus de Coveran was a witness to a document which confirmed the transfer of land from Dughall MacSuibhne (MacSween) to Walter Stewart, the Earl of Menteith. The land in question included Skipness Castle on the east side of the Kintyre Peninsula near the village of Skipness, Killislate and the parish of Kilcalmonell. The Earl then granted the church of Kilcalmonell to the monks of Paisley. Walter Stewart was the third son of the Lord High Steward of Scotland, who was the personal representative of the King of Scotland and, as such one of the most powerful men in the land. So Waldenus de Coveran was mixing in exalted company indeed.

Further proof of the family's VIP status came a few years later. By 1297 the family name had changed to Cochran and Baron William de Cochran was a signatory on King Edward's

Ragman Rolls. This was the name given to a collection of agreements, laid out on four rolls of parchment, which King Edward the first of England imposed on Scottish nobility and land-owners in return for deciding who should be the next king of Scotland.

The family continued to prosper, but there came a time when it almost died out. In common with most Scots they simplified their Norman name and became simply Cochran.

In 1576 William Cochrane of that Ilk was granted a charter by Queen Mary confirming his ownership of the lands of Cochran. He and his wife Margaret had only one child, a daughter, Elizabeth. In 1593, he named her as the sole heir of his estate. However he stipulated that her eventual husband would assume the name Cochrane. This duly came to pass when she married Alexander Blair, from Ayrshire.

Mr and Mrs Cochrane had seven sons and three daughters. The eldest son, Sir John Cochrane, was a colonel in the army of Charles the First. He was sent to solicit the assistance of foreign princes, and later by Charles the Second to run his embassy in Poland. He died, with no heirs. The estate passed to his brother, Sir William Cochrane of Cowdon, who in 1647 became Lord Cochrane of Ochiltree. In May 1669 he was elevated again and became the Earl of Dundonald, firmly establishing the Cochranes at the top end of Scotland's nobility.

Chapter three:

The architect
and the admiral

**Over the centuries the Cochranes have provided
a large number of colourful characters, who
left their mark on history.**

And none more so than Robert Cochrane
and Admiral Thomas Cochrane.

Robert was born in Scotland and educated
in Italy and rose to become one of fifteenth
century Scotland's most eminent architects. He
was employed by James the Third to design and
erect several royal buildings and such were his
skills and personality that he soon became a firm
favourite of the king. King James was unusual
because he decided against surrounding himself
with the nobility. Instead he preferred the likes of
architects, tradesmen and musicians as his closest
companions. Before long Robert Cochrane was
the king's closest and most trusted advisor. King

James even bestowed upon Cochrane the Earldom of Mar, a title that had previously belonged to the monarch's brother, John Boyd, who had been executed by James for trying to usurp his crown.

He became so powerful that any communication to the king had to be seen by him first. It was a position which opened him up to all sorts of bribes and it's understood he helped himself to a great many. He soon became wealthy beyond his wildest dreams, while the king turned a blind eye.

Cochrane felt he was untouchable and soon began to extend his power even further. One day he decided that the silver coin of the realm should be mixed with brass and lead. This reduced the currency's value, but Cochrane produced a proclamation instructing the populace that this new coin was equal in value to the old silver coin. This resulted in near anarchy when farmers refused to sell their produce for the new money. There was increasing pressure on Cochrane to return the currency to the old silver standard but he refused, saying, "The day I am hanged they may be called in; not sooner". It was meant to be a joke but those words came back to haunt him.

In July 1484 Scotland's nobility held a secret meeting to agree a way of ridding the country of the king's favourites. Cochrane heard about the get-together at the church in Lauder and in his arrogant manner marched up to the front door and insisted on being allowed in. He was accompanied by a guard of three hundred armed men, all dressed in his livery of white with black facings. Cochrane sported a black velvet riding suit with a gold chain round his neck and a golden bugle horn hanging from his side.

Sir Robert Douglas, of Lochleven, who was guarding the door, heard the knocking, demanded who was there. Cocbrane answered, "The Earl of Mar", and was allowed to enter.

As soon as he was inside he was attacked by a couple of Lords, one who grabbed the gold chain and pulled it off his neck and another who ripped off his bugle horn.

Cochrane was stunned by this behaviour and asked his assailants if they were jesting. But their Lordships were not kidding and furthermore warned Cochrane that he had been abusing his power for far too long and was now about to be punished.

At that point a deputation from the church went to the nearby camp of King James and snatched away his other cronies, whom they despised. They then condemned them to death for deliberately giving the king bad advice to the detriment of the whole country. Cochrane and his companions were then frog-marched to a nearby bridge and hanged.

Perhaps the most famous Cochrane of all was Thomas Cochrane whose roller-coaster life has been immortalized in several works of fiction. He was born near Hamilton in 1775 and his father was the ninth Earl of Dundonald.

His uncle, who became Admiral Sir Alexander Cochrane, was a major influence on his early life.

Alexander had him listed as a crew member on four Royal Navy ships from the age of five onwards. This was an illegal practice but a way of ensuring a head start for a youngster whose family hoped one day he would become a navy officer. And in 1793, in the midst of the French Revolution, he duly joined the Royal Navy.

Cochrane's first appointment was in the Baltic aboard HMS *Hind*, commanded by his uncle. Two years later, in 1795, he was promoted to acting lieutenant on HMS *Thetis*. However he still hadn't sat the lieutenant's exam so wasn't confirmed in the job. But in 1796 he passed and two years later was appointed eighth Lieutenant on Lord Keith's flagship, HMS *Barfleur* in the Mediterranean.

It was on this tour of duty that Cochrane's true personality first emerged. He was charged with allegedly disrespect to the ship's first lieutenant. After a court martial he was found not guilty. However, he was reprimanded for being flippant. Throughout his life Cochrane had difficulty relating to other people. He just couldn't get along with many of his superiors, subordinates, employers and colleagues in several navies and Parliament. This attitude led to a feud with John Jervis, 1st Earl of St Vincent, who was commander in chief of the Mediterranean fleet and a noted authoritarian.

In 1800, Cochrane was appointed to command the brig sloop HMS *Speedy* and displayed the amazing combination of enterprise and quick-thinking which would later lead him to fame and fortune.

Speedy was almost captured by a Spanish warship concealed as a merchant ship. Cochrane escaped by flying a Danish flag and dissuading an attempt to investigate by claiming his ship was plague-ridden.

The Spaniards continued to follow him through the night. Cochrane knew that if they got a good look at his ship in daylight the game would be up. So he placed a candle on a barrel and let it float away. The Spanish followed the candle and *Speedy* escaped. This was the world's first smokescreen.

A year later his mischevious nature got him into trouble again. He got into an argument with a French officer, which led to a duel.

Cochrane had turned up at a fancy dress ball on Malta dressed as a common sailor. The Frenchman obviously forgot it was fancy dress and treated Cochrane as if he were just a sailor, as opposed to an officer. It was pistols at dawn and, surprise surprise, Cochrane came off best. The Frenchman was hurt and Cochrane was not.

That same year another glorious chapter was added to his naval exploits. On May 6, 1801 off the coast of Barcelona he took the fight to the Spanish frigate *El Gamo*. The Spanish vessel was laden with 32 guns and 319 sailors. *Speedy* was equipped with just 14 cannons and 54 men. Cochrane flew an American flag to conceal his identity and get very close to the Spaniards. By the time they realized his deception he was too close to fire on. He approached so closely to *Gamo* that its guns could not fire on the *Speedy's* hull. This left only the option of boarding, but whenever the Spanish were on the verge of doing so Cochrane would drift away and fire his weapons on the boarding parties. The tactic wreaked havoc on the Spaniards and eventually it was Cochrane's men who boarded the enemy ship and took possession. In all, while in charge of *Speedy,* Cochrane accounted for more than 50 enemy ships in a 15-month period.

In 1803, St Vincent, with whom he was still feuding, put Cochrane in command of a captured French privateer, HMS *Arab* (formerly *Le Brave*). This was a way of punishing Cochrane for past misdemeanors, because *Arab* was a poorly designed vessel which was very difficult to maneouvre. So much so, it collided twice with Royal Navy ships, with Cochrane in charge. St Vincent continued to hound Cochrane and soon moved him with the *Arab* to fishing fleet protection duties in the North Sea.

In 1804, the new government of William Pitt the Younger removed St Vincent and Cochrane was appointed to command the 32-gun frigate HMS *Pallas*. Three years later he was given command of the 38-gun frigate *Imperieuse*. One of his midshipmen was Frederick Marryat who later wrote fictionalized accounts of his adventures with Cochrane.

Cochrane launched many a raid on the southern coast of France. During one such assault he found code books at a signal station. He copied them but left the originals behind to convince the French that their military secrets remained intact.

The French called him le loup des mers (The Sea Wolf) and at over six feet tall and with bright red hair, Cochrane was an imposing figure on the bridge. Thanks to meticulous planning he became one of the most daring and skilled captains of his generation. His tactics helped him and the men under his command earn fabulous bounties. While in charge of the *Pallas*, for example, he captured Spanish treasure ships and his personal reward was £75,000. However, he could not accept unfair action by his superiors and insisted on fighting these decisions. This definitely had a major negative impact on his progress in the Royal Navy.

In June 1806 he stood for parliament but lost. Four months later there was another election and this time he succeeded in becoming the MP for Honiton. It emerged some years later that, although he was publicly vehemently opposed to bribery for votes, he had paid ten guineas to each voter who chose him in the ballot. The cash was handled by an intermediary. Cochrane remained an MP for the next 12 years and was an outspoken criticism of the conduct of the war and corruption in the navy.

In 1812, Cochrane married Katherine Frances Corbet Barnes, who was more than 20 years younger than him. The couple had eloped and tied the knot in a civil ceremony. This enraged Cochrane's fabulously wealthy uncle who promptly disinherited him as a punishment.

The couple remarried in an Anglican church in 1818 and seven years later renewed their vows in the Church of Scotland. These ceremonies led to suspicions that Cochrane's first son, Thomas Barnes Cochrane, was illegitimate. But in 1831, on the death of his father, Thomas Cochrane became the 10th Earl Dundonald.

Cochrane had made many enemies, both in politics and in the navy and in 1814 they appeared to get their own back on him. Cochrane was named as a major suspect in an attempt to manipulate the London Stock Exchange. The Great Stock Exchange Fraud began with 'news', circulated by so-called French officers that Napoleon, with whom Britain was at war, had been killed. The bearers of these good tidings further stated that peace between England and France would now surely follow. The value of government securities rose rapidly on the back of these claims. However, a few hours later the government announced that the news about Napoleon's demise was either a hoax or a deliberate falsehood and prices fell back to their previous levels. The Stock Exchange launched an investigation and found that in excess of £1.1 million of two government-based stocks, most of it purchased the previous week, had been sold for great profit. Three people connected with that purchase were charged with the fraud. They were Lord Cochrane MP, his uncle the Hon. Andrew Cochrane-Johnstone, and Richard Butt, Lord Cochrane's financial advisor. All three were found guilty. They were sentenced to 12 months in prison, a fine of £1000 each, and an hour in the public pillory, which was a more severe form of the stocks. Lord Cochrane was also stripped of his naval rank and expelled from the Order of the Bath. He was thrown out of Parliament and a by-election was called.

Things looked bleak for Cochrane, but he continued to plead his innocence. Public opinion was behind him and many felt the trial judge had been biased against him. He comfortably won the by-election to get back in to the House of Commons and due to public outcry over his treatment, the punishment of the pillory was officially discontinued in Britain.

In 1832, after nearly 20 years of campaigning, he was granted a free pardon, including reinstatement to his rank of rear admiral. Restoration of the Order of the Bath and other honors followed and in 1877 a Select Committee decided that he was innocent.

However, prior to that there were several more twists to his amazing life story.

Cochrane left the UK in official disgrace

in 1818. At the request of Chilean leader Bernardo O'Higgins, he took command of the Chilean Navy in their war of independence against Spain.

He raided the coasts of Chile and Peru as he had France and Spain and introduced British naval customs into the Chilean navy. He organised and led the capture of Valdivia, Spain's most important base in Chile. Later, he led the Chilean navy in a series of battles to free Peru from Spain. In gratitude the Chileans named five navy ships after Admiral Cochrane. But that wasn't the end of his South American sojourn. He next successfully took charge of the Brazilian navy while they fought for independence from Portugal. Thanks to his successes he was created the Marquess of Maranham.

In 1860 Lord Thomas Cochrane twice underwent painful surgery for kidney stones. He died during the second one on October 31 and was buried in Westminster Abbey.

Apart from being a brilliant naval officer, Cochrane was also an inventor who designed among others the smokescreen, and the world's first weapon of mass destruction. His plans for poison gas were considered so dangerous, they were kept secret until 1908.

His exploits provided great material for a number of authors of naval fiction. The first was Captain Marryat who had served under him as a midshipman. In the 20th century, the fictional careers of Horatio Hornblower in the novels by C. S. Forester and of Jack Aubrey in the Aubrey–Maturin series of novels by Patrick O'Brian were modelled on his exploits. And the novel *The Sea Lord* (originally *The Frigate Captain*) by Showell Styles is about Lord Cochrane.

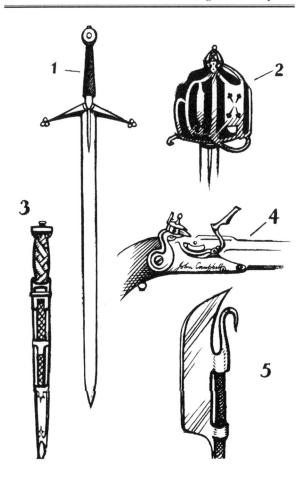

Highland weapons

1) The claymore or two-handed sword
   (fifteenth or early sixteenth century)

2) Basket hilt of broadsword
   made in Stirling, 1716

3) Highland dirk
   (eighteenth century)

4) Steel pistol *(detail)* made in Doune

5) Head of Lochaber Axe as carried
   in the '45 and earlier